Leveraging Social Media to Build Internationally Savvy Businesses

Table of Contents

We don't have a choice on whether we DO social media, the question is how well we DO it.

Chapter 1. Introduction

In the bustling digital landscape of the 21st century, businesses across the spectrum are awakened to the boundless potential of social media in burgeoning the globalization of their enterprises. Our Special Report unpacks the fascinating realm of "Leveraging Social Media to Build Internationally Savvy Businesses." Get ready to dive headfirst into an ocean of insightful knowledge, brimming with case studies, expert opinions, and meticulously curated strategies that will illuminate your pathway to global success. This report is your golden ticket to the enchanting world of global business success, helping your enterprise make friends with borders, smash language barriers and master the art of international customer engagement. Embrace a light-hearted journey, filled with intriguing and practical nuggets of wisdom, designed to catapult your business way beyond domestic shores into the unchartered territories of international accolades. This is not just another report - it's your globe-trotting virtual business companion!

Chapter 2. The Global Shift: Understanding Social Media's Place in Today's Business Landscape

In the electrifying ambiance of the primordial days of the 21st century, a powerful shift was underfoot, akin to the seismic transformation of the tectonic plates beneath our Earth. The hum of the internet became a roar, and the digital revolution, firmly rooted in the cyberscape, birthed an equally revolutionary platform for social communication: social media.

2.1. The Genesis of the Social Media Phenomenon

Perhaps it's worthwhile to stroll down memory lane to the genesis of this behemoth. In the late '90s and early 2000s, the internet was still an infant, staggering onto its feet, stretching its wings. Chat rooms and email lists were prevalent, providing a nascent indication of the social protuberance in the cyberspace. However, the launch of platforms like Friendster and MySpace was the clarion call of a new age. These platforms presented a cyberspace iteration of our social worlds, infusing a sense of tangibility into digital connections. The stage was set, and when Facebook arrived on February 4, 2004, a new epoch in human communication commenced. The term "social media" had officially made its entrance.

2.2. From Social Media to Business Media

Fast forward to a time when the social media phenomenon had expanded far beyond personal connections and casual communication. Companies started to latch onto its power, transforming these platforms into vibrant marketplaces. LinkedIn, launched in 2003, already offered the idea of an online professional networking platform. But the evolution of Facebook, Twitter, Instagram, and their ilk into advertising platforms marked a seismic global shift. Social media was not just a way for people to post their daily life updates, or for friends to connect across the globe; it had metamorphosed into an indispensable and nigh omnipresent part of the business landscape.

Businesses rushed to create online personas, sprouting digital billboards where once there were personal profiles. It became clear that social media offered a unique opportunity to engage with an audience much larger and diverse than any traditional media platform. From mammoth corporations to fledgling start-ups, every enterprise wanted a piece of the social media pie. Banner ads, sponsored posts, promotional videos, influencer partnerships - the tactics were varied but the goal was one - to leverage the reach and popularity of these platforms for business growth.

2.3. Social Media - A Global Connection

The usage of social media for business is not a phenomenon limited to a particular region or even restricted to the developed world. No, its allure is universal, permeating geographical boundaries, straddling economies, and binding the globe in a common thread. Social media's immense reach was bound to transcend borders. Sites like YouTube, Facebook, and Twitter boast of billions of users, originating from every nook and cranny of our planet. This has enabled businesses to connect and engage with international audiences, painting a vivid image of their brands onto the global canvas.

Simply put, platforms like Twitter, Facebook, LinkedIn, or Instagram permit businesses to virtually rub shoulders with their audience, regardless of how geographically dispersed they may be. They offer the means to not just share updates, but to truly communicate - to showcase their brand, to understand their audience, and to adapt their strategies accordingly in real-time. It's a connected world, and social media is the umbilical cord that joins businesses with their prospective consumers globally.

2.4. Looking Ahead - The Virtual Global Marketplace

While analyzing the contours of social media's influence on businesses, we can look towards e-commerce and online marketplaces as a sign of what's to come. Today, platforms like Amazon, Alibaba, and eBay function as global marketplaces, connecting buyers and sellers from across the globe. This marks a significant departure from the physical constraints of a geographical marketplace and embodies the boundless opportunities the digital world has to offer.

Likewise, social media platforms are increasingly becoming conduits for business transactions. Facebook Marketplace, Instagram Shops, and Pinterest's Shoppable Pins are indicative of this trend. These virtual marketplaces are not confined by concerns about physical boundaries or logistics, but rather, are focused on fostering a global community of consumers and sellers. It is an exciting development, showcasing the truly international nature of the social media-induced business landscape.

As we draw the curtain on this chapter, it's clear that social media's place in today's business landscape, while already significant, continues to grow and evolve. Its role as an international connector and global marketplace manifests the vast potential it harbours for businesses willing to seize the opportunity. Businesses that can ride this wave of digital transformation will be better placed to navigate the international waters of the global marketplace.

Chapter 3. Crossing Borders: Why a Global Presence Matters

In the dynamic realm of today's economy, having an international presence is no longer just an additive advantage; it is a necessity. Expanding your business beyond domestic borders holds numerous advantages that enrich a business's operations, its brand image, and its overall standing in the competitive market landscape.

3.1. The Sunrise of Global Commerce

The unprecedented march of technology has shrunk our world to the extent that markets, which were once physically distant, are now only a click away. The concept of global commerce has thus taken flight like the proverbial phoenix, with technology acting as the wind beneath its wings. The market, once limited to geographical constraints, has metamorphosed into a vast, seemingly limitlessly accessible global marketplace, owing to the prodigious rise of E-Commerce and the digitization of trade. This transformation allows businesses to cast their nets wider and deeper, reaching consumers who were once beyond their grasp.

In today's vastly interconnected business arena, your potential customer could be sitting halfway around the globe, waiting to discover your products or services. The key to tapping into these untapped markets lies in utilizing the immense potential of tools like social media, which integrate the world into a single, compact hub of consumers, suppliers, collaborators, and competitors.

3.2. Magnifying Brand Influence

Casting a wide net, however, is just the tip of the iceberg. Embracing an international presence also contributes majorly towards amplifying your brand's overall influence. When your business appears on a global platform, interacting seamlessly with a diverse range of customers and stakeholders, it immediately appears more reliable and influential. This global credibility institutes trust, forges stronger customer relationships, and enhances the overall brand image in a way that a purely domestic presence would struggle to achieve.

Moreover, becoming a global player also paves the way for increased visibility and recognition which, in turn, aids greatly in attracting new customers while retaining existing ones. This increases the likelihood of your brand being recommended through word-of-mouth - the most authentic form of marketing there is. Consequently, a business that forays into the international market is likely to witness enhanced customer loyalty and gain a competitive edge in the market.

3.3. Diversifying Revenue Streams

Another compelling reason to embrace the global marketplace lies in the prospect of diversifying revenues. Operating in multiple markets around the world allows your business to tap into diverse consumer bases, thereby helping to spread the risk. Economic downturns, political instabilities, or even market saturation in one region could significantly impact your revenues if you are only operating in domestic realms. However, if your business has a global presence, the resultant diversified customer base can act as a buffer, mitigating against shocks in any particular market and providing a more stable financial foundation.

Further, international markets often present untapped opportunities, enabling businesses to discover new avenues for their products or services. It's akin to finding uncharted territories that are ripe for your business offerings, a chance to broaden your horizon beyond the familiar and explore the stimulating unknown.

3.4. Fostering Innovation and Growth

Operating in a global market can also infuse your business with a culture of innovation. When your business crosses the borders, it comes face-to-face with a range of different challenges, experiences, and demands. This melting pot of varied consumer needs, market conditions, and regulatory challenges can serve as an engine for innovation, forcing your business to adapt, improvise, and innovate - elements that are absolutely vital for any business to stay ahead of the competition and continuously evolve.

Whether it's tailoring your products to suit local tastes, tweaking your marketing strategies for better resonance, or even innovating in terms of logistics and distribution to fit the unique demands of each market, international business operations almost always prove to be a catalyst for growth and innovation.

In conclusion, having a global presence in today's market is not just an optional strategy; it is a powerhouse that can turbo-charge your business towards achieving new heights. It can open up avenues to new customer bases, diversify risks, magnify brand influence, and foster innovation and growth. As we continue to delve deeper into the realms of social media and globalization, businesses need to awaken to the potent combination of both, to thrive, and potentially lead, in the cosmopolitan future of international commerce.

Chapter 4. Building Your Social Media Strategy for Global Impact

In the cacophonic yet melodious ensemble of digital interactions, the harmony of robust social media strategies often underpin the success story of businesses aiming for international recognition. In order to comprehend and consequently ideate a successful strategy for global impact, businesses need to extend their understanding beyond local contexts and embrace the distinct attributes of diverse geographical regions.

4.1. Understanding International Social Media Landscapes

Before you venture on this exhilarating journey of building a universal digital footprint, the primary stepping stone is to comprehend the diverse landscapes of international social media platforms. Different countries have different preferred social media platforms, deeming a one-size-fits-all approach ineffective. Adequate research on the most heavily frequented platforms across your target countries can lead to an informed and more pointed approach to international social media marketing. Utilize dependable sources to gather data about social media utilization and preferences across different nations. This research should nestle the essence of your global social media strategy.

4.2. Tools and Techniques For Success

A treasure trove of tools and techniques lies at your disposal, waiting to be deployed to optimize your international social media strategy. Social Listening Tools like Hootsuite, Buffer or Sprout Social can aid you in understanding what global consumers are talking about, their concerns, and what they feel about your brand. Furthermore, Social Scheduling Tools can ensure that your messages reach different corners of the world at the right time, while Analytics Tools can provide insights into your performance and the impact of your social media campaigns.

4.3. Localization And Mastering Content Adaptation

One crucial parameter of a successful global social media strategy is the ability to adapt and localize your content. This extends past mere linguistic translation and includes understanding cultural nuances, consumer behavior, local holidays, and more. The more tailored your approach to a specific market, the better your chances of resonating with the local audience and fostering meaningful connections.

4.4. Community Building and Audience Engagement

In this era of digital intimacy, it is paramount that your social media strategy prioritizes audience engagement. Creating a virtual space where your consumers feel heard, valued, and engaged can go a long way in building your brand loyalty and community. Hosting live interactive sessions, Q&As, coming up with creative engagement campaigns can boost your international social media presence.

4.5. Crisis Management Plan

While a robust strategy prepares you for success, it must also account for potential missteps. Social media faux pas can have unprecedented repercussions on your brand image, especially in the sensitive international market. Crafting a crisis management plan allows your business to respond promptly and efficiently to social media crises, mitigating the damage.

4.6. Measuring Success: Metrics And KPIs

Determining the right Key Performance Indicators (KPIs) is paramount in measuring your global strategy's success. Depending on your business strategy, KPIs could range from engagement metrics such as likes, shares, or comments, to metrics that directly impact your bottom line such as lead generation, conversion rates, or ROI.

Remember, a 'like' in the digital world may not directly convert to 'likeness' or loyalty in the real world. It's essential to measure metrics that align with your business objectives, and continuously optimize your social media strategy based on these insights.

As we traverse into the abyss of global social media, let's remember that continuous learning, unlearning, and adapting are the steeds of success. The digital landscape is ephemeral and dynamic, and so must be your social media strategies. Embrace the change and propel your business into digital stardom. There are countless territories out there, waiting to hear your brand's story, and if you tell it right, they wouldn't hesitate to adopt it as their own. After all, isn't adoption the first step to adaptation?

Chapter 5. Language and Culture: Breaking Barriers in International Markets

In the intricate labyrinth of international business, language and culture hold paramount importance. These elements drive communication, foment trust, express personality, and fundamentally shape the human experience in a business context. To triumph in foreign markets, businesses must capitalize on the power of language and unlock the potential imbedded within cultural subtleties. This pursuit shapes long-lasting relationships and fosters a resonating sense of belonging among international clients.

5.1. Navigating the Linguistic Landscape

Language is the conduit by which human experiences are richly painted, fostering understanding and manifesting our deepest ideas, intentions, and emotions. In an international business context, language doesn't simply involve translation from one language to another. It is a complex system of understanding embedded cultural nuances, dialects, slang, and references to mould your brand's communication strategies accordingly.

Every tongue sings a unique melody and mastering this symphony is crucial for international engagement. Adopting effective localization strategies goes beyond mere translation; it encapsulates the fine art of blending with the local linguistic culture. Localization is the rendition of your communication strategy to resonate with the local audience in their native language tones, connecting deeper with their emotions, and expressing respect for their cultural norms. Businesses must focus on the right language balance, keeping together the essence of the original message and adapting to local culture.

5.2. The Cultural Conundrum

Culture is a multi-hued tapestry, a melange of traditions, beliefs, customs, and societal norms that shape people's behaviors and interactions. Cultural sensitivity is a prerequisite for any business hoping to make inroads into international markets. Neglecting the cultural facets of a region can lead to costly errors, misinterpretations, or worse—it could offend your intended audience, devastating your brand's reputation and future prospects.

Businesses need to integrate cultural intelligence into their social media strategies to avoid fallout. To simplify, this includes understanding the local holidays, avoiding content that could be considered offensive or inappropriate, and incorporating elements of local culture, such as idioms, folklore, or colloquial language into posts. These seemingly minute details can delight the local audience, creating a strong bond with the brand.

5.3. The Power of Cultural Adaptation in Social Media

Cultural adaptation is not a one-size-fits-all design. The use of social media across different cultures often varies based on multiple factors such as societal norms, technological adoption rates, and language, to name a few. One culture's approach to social media can greatly differ from another, and understanding these differences is critical for social media success.

Consider the contrast between the heavily text-based Western social platforms vs. China's multimedia-dense Weibo or WeChat. A business that understands these contrasts is more likely to create content that resonates with the local populace, thereby leveraging the power of cultural adaptation.

5.4. The Quest for Cultural Analysis and Adaptation

To truly permeate a foreign market, companies must seek a profound understanding of cultural sensitivities. This journey begins with a thorough cultural analysis, incorporating elements of sociocultural, economic, legal, political, and technological aspects of a community. Employing native cultural experts adds value in navigating these subtle dimensions efficiently.

After analysis comes the stage of adaptation – transferring the understandings drawn into actionable strategies. On social media, this step involves creating and curating content that resonates with the regional culture and language. Adopting popular local trends or partnering with regional influencers could augment the business's social media outreach in the target market.

5.5. Stories of Cultural Adaptation - When Localization Wins

When brands align cultural intelligence with their social media strategy, international success stories are born. For example, successful global organizations like Coca-Cola, McDonald's, and Airbnb have adopted cultural adaptation to thrive in international markets. They illustrate that through effective navigation of language and culture; businesses can create a strong, lasting global footprint.

In conclusion, there are no shortcuts to breaking barriers in international markets. Exploring the uncharted waters of language and culture requires patience, sensitivity, and an open mind. While challenging, the rewards are immense, paving the road to lucrative markets and the hearts of millions of new customers. Mastering language and cultural intricacies can stand as the cornerstone of global business successes, uniting different worlds under the umbrella of mutual understanding, respect, and shared experiences. The charm of language and the beauty of cultural diversity, blended with a well-crafted social media strategy, can become a passport to international business triumph.

Chapter 6. Worldwide Engagement: Mastering Interaction on Global Platforms

Mastering interaction on global platforms isn't a walk in the park. It's an intricate dance that needs rhythm, precision, and most importantly, an understanding of the dance floor. Your dance floor, in this context, is the culminated reality of the digital properties where your business chooses to engage.

6.1. Engaging on Different Social Media Platforms

When you join a social media platform, you essentially become a resident. And like any responsible resident, you have to respect the culture of the platform. Facebook, with its over 2.7 billion users, may seem like a goldmine of a market. But bear in mind, not all of them are your prospective customers. Identifying and engaging with your target audience in this vast sea of users requires a meticulously curated strategy and a specific tone of communication.

Twitter, on the other hand, thrives on the pulse of the present. If you blink, you miss. It boasts real-time, chronological conversations that move at a blistering pace. Catering to an audience who are not only just tweeting but also retweeting, replying, liking, following, and unfollowing can be quite a challenge. Your tweets need to be razor-sharp, timely, and constantly flowing. The investment here is not just in crafting compelling content but also in being ready to engage with the ongoing discourse.

Meanwhile, Instagram rules the visual realm, attracting a younger demographic with its aesthetics-rich environment. Posts with eye-catching visuals, well-defined narratives, and strategic use of hashtags define the Instagram engagement playbook.

LinkedIn, the professional networking site, demands a significantly different approach. Here, users are not looking to be sold to; they're searching for information, networking possibilities, and valuable insights.

6.2. Accessibility and Engagement

Accessibility is crucial for international engagement. Your social media pages need to be user-friendly and inclusive. Incorporating accessibility features like alternate text descriptions for images, subtitles for videos, and clear copy with easy-to-read font can make a difference in your interaction with an international audience.

Engagement is not merely about responding to likes, shares and comments on your posts. It also includes keeping track of mentions and tags, acknowledging user-generated content, and promptly dealing with customer concerns and queries. In essence, it's about building an active and responsive online community.

6.3. The Art of Interaction

Interacting on social media platforms means merging into the flow of existing conversations, sparking new ones, and always leaving room for more dialogues to follow. It's idolizing the mantra of "speak, listen, and learn." Guide your audience with carefully curated content, listen to their needs and feedback, and learn how to improve your strategy.

6.4. Listening to Your Audience

Ignoring your customers' voices on social media is like shooting yourself in the foot. Your audience is your critic, your cheerleader, your guide. From compliments and complaints to suggestions and queries, they give shape to your brand online. Listen to them, resolve their concerns, and grow from their feedback.

6.5. Semantic Analyses on Global Scale

Digging deeper into the realm of social media interaction, semantic analysis can be instrumental. This involves understanding the tone, context, and emotions behind your audience's comments and posts. Implementing semantic analysis on a global scale can require specialized language processing tools and dedicated teams, but the insights you'll gather are worth the effort.

6.6. Evaluating Engagement Success

Measuring your engagement success is more than just observing your number of likes or followers. You need to track shares, comments, mentions, impressions, click-through rates, and more. These metrics, combined with audience feedback and conversion rates, yield a holistic view of your social media engagement impact.

In conclusion, successfully mastering interaction on global platforms demands adaptable, empathetic, and proactive engagement. Decoding the unique cultures of different platforms and fostering an accessible, inclusive, and responsive environment pave the pathway for a thriving international presence. Building authentic relationships with your international audience will translate into sustainable engagement, leading to a profound impact on your brand's global footprint.

Chapter 7. Tales of Triumph: Case Studies in International Social Media Success

Something resonates in the depths of our souls when we hear stories of triumph. They captivate us, inspire us, and instill in us an insatiable hunger to achieve similar successes. In a world that is fast becoming a global village, it's no surprise that business triumphs are drawing the world's attention on the colossal stage of social media. Let's explore together the unparalleled victories of businesses that have ridden the waves of social media glory, serenaded the hearts of international customers, and transformed this digital tool into a golden ticket to global success.

7.1. The Global Takeover of Airbnb

Airbnb stands as an emblematic case of a localized US-based business breaking its chrysalis to become a truly international butterfly. This online marketplace started operating as an air mattress rental system for conferences in San Francisco, but its rise to global ubiquity is a testament to its innovative, intriguing, and highly engaging social media strategy.

In addition to its staple blend of captivating images, Airbnb effectively employed user-generated content from hosts around the world to make their advertisements more authentic. They initiated the #LiveThere campaign on Instagram and Twitter, encouraging users to share their experiences of 'living like a local', thereby weaving their personal narratives into the greater Airbnb story. From featuring picturesque locations to unexplored city corners, Airbnb's social media content thrived on the elements of surprise and discovery, sparking imagination and wanderlust in their audience spanning 220+ countries and regions. Although they faced regulatory hurdles in several countries, the strength of their community-building strategies on social media ensured they maintained a reassuring rapport with their international user base.

7.2. Domino's Pizza's Crust of Success Is Digital

Domino's Pizza evolved from being a beleaguered pizza brand in the US to a proudly global entity fostering a digital-first culture. They recognized the increasing power of social media early and pivoted their entire business strategy, thereby catalyzing their astounding rise in the international market.

Domino's leveraged social media to connect directly with customers, encouraging them to dish out feedback and playing cleverly with customer feedback hashtags like #pizzarewards and #easyorder. Domino's game-changing step was the introduction of the 'AnyWare' campaign that allowed customers to order pizza via social media platforms. This decision transformed user experience and bolstered its brand image as a tech-savvy pizza brand. The impact of such an innovative marketing strategy is evident in Domino's remarkable turnaround: from struggling with declining sales to becoming a global behemoth lining up nearly 17,000 stores in more than 90 countries.

7.3. Spotify's Melodious Stride Into Global Markets

Another triumphant tale of social media success is that of Spotify. This music-streaming powerhouse with origins in Sweden has masterfully tuned its global social media strategy to resonate with cultural nuances in diverse markets.

Spotify artistically employed data-driven storytelling by unveiling the annual Wrapped campaign. The campaign presented listeners with personalized summaries of their year in music, leading to a massive surge in user engagement across social media. Users were eager to share their musical journey, making Wrapped an organic and authentic marketing coup. Spotify also skillfully used local influencer endorsements and spotlighted regional artists to engage with local cultures and customs. Their social media strategy reflected an astute understanding of global markets, helping Spotify reach over 345 million active monthly users in around 170 markets worldwide.

These tales of triumph help us appreciate the transformative potential of social media in scaling businesses globally. They serve as a rich source of inspiration for entrepreneurs and businesses who envision a future beyond borders. Each story is a compendium of wisdom, a testament to adaptability, agility, and a relentless pursuit of customer engagement on an international level. Their journey, laid with strategic social media maneuvers, underscores the power of digital platforms to resonate with cultures worldwide, connect continents, and create lasting global impressions. So, as you begin to chart your own international social media strategy, remember - a globally loved brand is but a tweet, a post, or a share away.

Remember, Dear reader, these tales of triumph are not exceptions; they're examples of what could be achieved with thoughtful planning, adaptability, and a customer-centric approach on the global stage of social media. You too can write a chapter in your business's international social media success. As a popular adage goes: where success is concerned, 'Sky is not the limit, it's just the view.' It's your turn to reach for the stars, guided by these tales of triumph.

Chapter 8. Risk and Rewards: The Dark Side of Going Global on Social Media

It is often said, "With great power comes great responsibility." The advent of social media has undoubtedly bestowed upon businesses a powerful tool for global expansion. However, this tool doesn't come without its set of perils. Its pervasiveness and ease of access make it both an implement of progress and potentially a weapon of self-destruction. Failing to accurately gauge and mitigate the risks involved might lead to negative repercussions that could detrimentally affect the business's reputation.

8.1. The Unfurling Landscape of Digital Risks

Operating within the global digital space inevitably exposes businesses to a rich web of interconnected risks. These include cyber threats, misinformation, regulatory breaches, and cultural faux pas, just to name a few. Cyber threats, in particular, are rampant, thanks to technological advancements and the ubiquity of digital channels. From phishing scams and data breaches to disruptive attacks on a company's social media pages, the haunting spectrum of digital threats looms large.

Misinformation or disinformation campaigns can be particularly problematic for businesses leveraging social media. A single false statement or misleading accusation can spiral into a damaging narrative that's difficult to control and could devastate a business's hard-earned reputation. Regulatory breaches can occur when businesses, particularly those expanding their reach globally, unknowingly fail to comply with certain regulations, like data privacy laws, laid down by the countries they operate in. A business must remain vigilant about these laws and standards to avoid any potential legal fallout.

Finally, there is the risk of a cultural faux pas. Businesses taking their first steps in new international markets can sometimes fail to understand the cultural sensitivities and social norms native to their target demographic. Such a mistake may harm the brand's image and make the market entry far more difficult than intended.

8.2. Treading the Fine Line: Balancing Risk and Reward

Every business, while formulating its international social media strategy, should consciously strive to maintain a delicate balance between the potential risks and rewards. Identifying potential pain points and being able to respond rapidly and effectively is crucial to this endeavor. The key lies in forethought – predicting possible risks, estimating their impacts and probabilities, and mixing these ingredients into the strategic planning brew.

Moreover, businesses should create a crisis management plan - a guide that lays out the series of actions to be taken when things go awry. Several aspects of this are critical. Its scope should cover all probable incidents, and the adequacy of resources (both human and financial) to deal with such contingencies should be ensured. A concerted communication strategy, as part of a crisis management plan, could be the difference between an effective damage limitation and a full-scale public relations disaster.

8.3. Navigating the Cyber Threat Abyss

In the event of a cyber threat, businesses need to ensure that they have robust security measures in place. This includes secure data management systems, strong privacy protocols, and regular audits to test and bolster the robustness of these measures. Additionally, businesses should equip their employees with knowledge and tools to detect and deal with cyber threats.

Third-party cybersecurity firms can be employed to test the business's digital fortifications using programs like ethical hacking. Should a data breach occur, swift action is paramount. Notifying affected stakeholders, identifying and rectifying security loopholes, and handling communication delicately and transparently can attenuate the damage.

8.4. Correcting the Narrative: Combatting Misinformation

Misinformation can be a tricky field to navigate. However, early detection and swift responses can often stem the tide. Social media listening tools can be used to monitor online chatter about the business and flag potentially damaging narratives. Once identified, fact-based, clear, and emphatic communication can help to dispel misapprehensions and realign the narrative saying otherwise.

8.5. Conforming to Global Standards: Regulatory Compliance

To avoid falling foul of international regulations, businesses should invest time and resources to understand the legal landscape of their global markets. Legal counsel, either internal or from a consultancy, should be employed to ensure that the business's social media activities align with the relevant laws and standards of the countries of operation.

8.6. Respecting Cultural Nuances

Respecting and understanding local cultural nuances is indispensable. Localizing content to suit cultural eccentricities can, in fact, double up as a secret weapon helping businesses to win the hearts of their target demographic. Investing in local talent, seeking regional collaboration and partnerships, and soliciting feedback from the local audience can greatly assist in this endeavor.

8.7. Overcoming the Dark Side

In conclusion, going global on social media is indeed a tightrope walk. The risks are numerous and often unpredictable. It's crucial to appreciate that while rewards beckon, wisdom lies in acknowledging and preparing for the potential pitfalls. The emphasis should always be on early detection, fast response times, well-conceived strategies, and a transparent communication approach on all fronts. The more businesses adhere to these principles, the better equipped they will be to harness the power of social media for global expansion, turning potential stumbling blocks into stepping stones towards international success.

Chapter 9. Global Compliance: Legal and Ethical Aspects of International Social Media

The explosion of social media and its subsequent economical ubiquity on the global stage has presented businesses with an unprecedented medium for international growth. However, with these opportunities to widen scopes and scales of operation, also come a unique set of challenges. One of the most salient challenges is ensuring that a business's global digital presence adheres to the legal and ethical guidelines of each region of operation. This, often complex, dance between the thirst for international presence and complying with complex, myriad, and potentially contradicting regulatory laws, is both an art and a science that must be mastered by corporations seeking success beyond their domestic jurisdictions.

9.1. The Global Regulatory Environment

Around the world, diverse countries have distinct laws and regulations surrounding the use of social media. These range from data privacy laws, advertising regulations, to extremely specific rules about aspects such as content and timings of posts. Organizations must stay updated with these rules, which are dynamic and shift contour regularly to keep pace with the rapidly evolving digital landscape. Ignorance about, or negligence to adhere to these regulations could result in severe penalties and can tarnish a brand's reputation almost irreversibly.

For instance, the EU's General Data Protection Regulation (GDPR) mandates stringent requirements for the collection, processing, and storage of personal data. Violations can result in hefty penalties – up to 4% of the company's global annual turnover or €20 million, whichever is greater. Similar regulations exist in different jurisdictions like the Personal Data Protection Act in Singapore, or the Federal Law on Protection of Personal Data in Mexico. Understanding and adapting to these regulations becomes crucial for businesses expanding their digital footprint.

9.2. Ethical Considerations

Beyond the black and white domain of legal compliance, lie the grey areas of ethical conduct. In today's hyper-aware and conscientious society, businesses are expected to uphold a certain set of ethical standards - a failure to do so can lead to severe backlash, even if no laws are technically breached. Ethical considerations could involve respecting cultural sensitivities, maintaining consumer confidentiality, and ensuring transparent communication. Businesses must foster a culture of respect, were accurate representation of peoples, places, and customs, is not an afterthought but an intrinsic value of the company's global social media strategy.

One example could be clothing giant H&M's controversial ad featuring a black child wearing a sweater that said, "Coolest Monkey in the Jungle". While there might not have been legal ramifications, the lack of cultural and societal sensitivity resulted in widespread global outrage, impacting the brand both reputationally and financially.

9.3. Setting up Compliance Frameworks

Preparing for these challenges requires systematic approaches. Companies should establish a clear, comprehensive, cross-functional compliance framework enveloping legal and ethical aspects, emphasizing robust oversight and prompt response to changing laws and emerging ethical issues.

The process could be kickstarted by conducting a comprehensive audit of all likely legal and ethical issues that could arise. It might be beneficial to involve stakeholders from diverse areas such as legal, marketing, PR and HR in this process. Once risks are identified, businesses should develop strategies to mitigate them. This could involve training teams on global compliance issues or investing in tools to manage data privacy.

9.4. The Power of Localisation

Finally, businesses must understand that there is no one-size-fits-all strategy for global compliance. Just as a company would adjust its marketing strategy to cater to the regional tastes, so too must its compliance strategies be customized to reflect the specific laws and cultural nuances of each operating location. This allows businesses not only to avoid legal and ethical pitfalls but also helps synchronize their conduct with their global audience's expectations – and such alignment with customer preferences can only be good for business.

Localisation could involve steps like consulting with local legal experts to understand regional laws and regulations, employing or consulting with native or local social media managers to grasp cultural nuances in content creation, and ensuring there's a system for prompt updates and adaptations to any changes in law or cultural sentiments.

Ultimately, global compliance in international social media entails navigating a labyrinth of legal systems and cultural disparities and doing so with grace, humility, and respect. While this might pose a formidable challenge, businesses equipped with the right understanding and strategic initiatives will find that the rewards, reputationally and financially, vastly outweigh the intricacies of the journey. For, in today's interconnected digital age, a proactive approach to global compliance isn't just a legal necessity – it's a business imperative.

Chapter 10. Building a Global Brand: Harnessing the Power of Social Media

The concept of brand building appears as a near-ubiquitous chant in the rhythmic humdrum of contemporary business strategy. No matter the industry, size, or even the longevity of the enterprise, the need for a persuasive and distinctive brand persona resonates broadly with unequivocal and enduring significance. Thus, the task at hand is not just about merely building a brand - it's about architecting and nurturing a brand with an unwavering globally-resonant voice, in an arena where change is the only constant – social media.

10.1. Branding in a Digital Stratosphere

In the digital age, branding bears far greater layers of complexity and dynamism compared to its traditional counterpart. Here, brands don't exist merely as stationary logos, slogans, or corporate colors; instead, they present themselves as living, evolving entities that communicate, engage, and develop relationships. They transcend the physical boundaries embedded in their products or services to personify values, sentiments, stories, experiences.

With social media as the canvas, brands metamorphose into social entities. They, like any social being, have personalities, have values, have voices, and have stories. As a result, they possess the power of sentiment, engagement, influence, and virality, which are all foundational to the growth and globalization of a brand in today's industrial landscape.

10.2. The Role of Social Media in Global Brand Building

Many would agree that the advent of social media is a boon for brands. With numerous platforms at their disposal, brands now have access to reach a stupendously large and diverse audience base at the click of a button. What makes these platforms so potent for brands are:

- Interactivity: Brands can engage one-on-one with their audience, making the relationship more personal and authentic.

- Speed: Social media allows brands to communicate instantaneously. Information spreads rapidly, intensifying the growth and reach of the brand.

- Analytics: With direct insight into audience behavior and preferences, brands can tailor their persona to match their target demographic.

- Cost-effectiveness: Compare it to traditional media and you'll see that social media offers a much more cost-effective solution for brands to showcase their identity.

10.3. Building Your Brand's Social Media Strategy

The next step, of course, is leveraging these strengths of social media to foster an international brand image. This is less about random posts and more about a meticulously crafted strategy that takes into account the unique dynamics of various platforms, content types, and audience segments.

1. Understand your Audience: Your brand is not for you, but for your audience. Thus, it is vital to understand who they are, what they want and how they think. Use analytics to unravel their

psyche.

2. Define a clear Brand Message: Your brand's message is the backbone of your brand persona. Ensure it resonantly echoes across all platforms uniformly, to maintain consistency.

3. Create engaging content: Use different styles - storytelling, humor, inspiration, knowledge, surprise - to keep your audience engaged and intrigued.

4. Network: Collaborate with influencers, other brands, and your audience themselves to not just increase your brand reach but also build a community.

5. Listen and Respond: Keep a weather eye on the feedback and respond actively, showing that you care.

10.4. The Journey from Local to Global

Building an international brand image through social media is not a feat accomplished overnight. It demands persistence, patience, and continuous learning where the brand must evolve as an international entity, understanding and respecting the diverse cultural nuances of its global audience. It's a thorny path indeed, fraught with challenges and pitfalls; but the rewards - global recognition, immense growth, international customer loyalty - make the journey unquestionably worthwhile.

Trial and error couple with innovation and adaptation to pave the way forward. Moreover, brands must not lose sight of their primary vision and values, for it's their unique persona that will set them apart on the international stage.

With the right social media strategy, brands can navigate the potential minefield and emerge victorious as a global brand entity, reaching the hearts and minds of consumers worldwide. The power of social media in brand building is immense, and those who can harness it are the ones that will lead in the ever-connected world of the 21st century. Embrace the journey, and witness your brand evolve, inspire and thrive across borders and across hearts.

Chapter 11. The Future of International Business and Social Media: Emerging Trends and Predictions

At the interstice of the international business sphere and the dynamic world of social media lies an evolving landscape, vibrant with possibilities and riddled with challenges. Embarking on this journey of exploration, we glean insights, expectations, and intelligent projections, ensnaring our attention with the allure of the unknown yet probable.

11.1. The Marriage of Global Commerce and Social Media

In the fluid world we inhabit, the asynchrony between technology and traditional business norms is disappearing swiftly. A synergism is taking place - a marriage, if you will, of international commerce and social media. This merger is not just a shallow infatuation; instead, it bespeaks of a deep-seated fusion, one poised to completely disrupt the foreseeable future of global business operations.

The mechanics of global commerce is being reshaped by the powerful influence of social media. The conversion of interactions into transactions, the blurring lines between consumer and influencer, the democratization of marketplace power – all these underline the profound impact that social media has on global enterprises. Enhanced brand visibility, speedy customer service, targeted advertising, and real-time feedback are only the crest of the tidal wave that is revolutionizing the world of business.

11.2. Disruptive Technologies: A Chaotic Harmony

The future of international businesses and social media resides in disruptive technologies. Artificial intelligence, machine learning, big data, blockchain, and the Internet of Things form the quintet of disruptors positioned to revolutionize the global marketplace.

Each serves as a crucial cog in the hefty machinery of enterprise digital transformation. Unearthed data provides business insights of unprecedented depth. AI forges improvements in customer service via intelligent bots. Blockchain promises enhanced security measures, while IoT amplifies the connectedness of consumers and businesses.

These technologies harmonize in a symphony of scalability, integration, and automation to redefine the business landscape. This chaotic harmony dwells in the potential industries are keen to unleash.

11.3. Content Evolution: The Rise of Video and Immersive Experiences

Textual content, while invaluable, has come face to face with innovative challengers in the arena of social media dominance. The rise of video and immersive experiences is a paradigm shift hard to ignore. Video platforms, virtual reality, augmented reality, and interactive content form an enticing multimedia spectrum attracting the global audience in droves.

This seismic shift from text to visually rich content is fueled by increased mobile penetration, higher internet speeds, and enhanced consumer engagement with interactive content. Businesses are now leveraging these trends, churning out creative, engaging, and personalized content for their international audiences.

11.4. The Ethos of Personalization: Terminus of the Customer Journey

Riding the wave of technological advancements, businesses are now endowed with tools to tailor-make experiences for consumers, shaping the future of customer digitized journeys. By harnessing machine learning algorithms and big data analysis, businesses can create poignant, individualized communication, impactfully engaging customers across geographies.

Lingering on the horizon is the ethos of personalization, transforming bland, one-size-fits-all marketing plans into vibrant, culturally-aware, customer-focused global strategies. In this ultramodern narrative, the customer is no longer the endpoint but the epicenter of business strategies.

11.5. The Immutable Influence of Ethical and Legal Compliance

Possibly the most significant factor to ink its influence on the future of global business and social media is ethical and legal compliance. As businesses cross boundaries, they navigate through diverse regulatory environments, each with its unique set of laws, ethical standards, and cultural norms.

Issues like data privacy, fraud prevention, censorship, and intellectual property rights will continue to dominate the arena of global social media influences while shaping its trajectory. Compliances like GDPR in the EU, the Californian Consumer Privacy Act, and China's tight controls over web content provide blueprints for future discussions on regulations. Ultimately, businesses must juggle maximizing their social media outreach while ensuring stringent adherence to regional and international laws.

11.6. Embracing Change, Forging the Future

The grandeur of the predicted trends notwithstanding, the final lesson to be drawn from these predictions is not just adaptations to particular trends but the development of a more agile, future-ready business model. The momentum of change ignited by social media shows no signs of slowing, spelling a clear message for international businesses – those that are ready to pivot are those most likely to prevail.

In closing, the international business world and social media landscape are set to metamorphose and mutate, driven by technological advancements and transcultural integration. For businesses globally, from established conglomerates to budding startups, the ability to change, adapt, and grow amidst this volatility will determine their place in the future chronicles of global business.

www.ingramcontent.com/pod-product-compliance
Lightning Source LLC
Chambersburg PA
CBHW071046260726
48661CB00007B/3170